anythink

NATURE'S MYSTERIES

ORGANISMS THAT GLOW

BOBI MARTIN

Britannica
Educational Publishing

IN ASSOCIATION WITH

ROSEN
EDUCATIONAL SERVICES

Published in 2017 by Britannica Educational Publishing (a trademark of Encyclopædia Britannica, Inc.) in association with The Rosen Publishing Group, Inc. 29 East 21st Street, New York, NY 10010

Distributed exclusively by Rosen Publishing.
To see additional Britannica Educational Publishing titles, go to rosenpublishing.com.

First Edition

Britannica Educational Publishing
J.E. Luebering: Executive Director, Core Editorial
Mary Rose McCudden: Editor, Britannica Student Encyclopedia

Rosen Publishing
Shalini Saxena: Editor
Nelson Sá: Art Director
Michael Moy: Designer
Cindy Reiman: Photography Manager
Karen Huang: Photo Researcher

Library of Congress Cataloging-in-Publication Data

Names: Martin, Bobi, author.
Title: Organisms that glow / Bobi Martin.
Description: First edition. | New York : Britannica Educational Publishing in
  association with The Rosen Publishing Group, Inc., 2017. | 2017 | Series:
  Nature's mysteries | Audience: Grades 1-4._ | Includes bibliographical
  references and index.
Identifiers: LCCN 2015044793| ISBN 9781680484823 (library bound : alk. paper)
  | ISBN 9781680484908 (pbk. : alk. paper) | ISBN 9781680484595 (6-pack :
  alk. paper)
Subjects: LCSH: Bioluminescence—Juvenile literature. |
  Biofluorescence—Juvenile literature.
Classification: LCC QH641 .M274 2017 | DDC 572.4358—dc23
LC record available at http://lccn.loc.gov/2015044793

Manufactured in the United States of America

CONTENTS

LIGHT MAKERS

From fireworks to light sticks, we love things that shine in the dark. So does nature! Did you know that hundreds of living **organisms** can glow? These plants and animals turn the chemical energy stored in their tissues into light. This is called bioluminescence (pronounced bye-oh-loo-muh-nes-uhns). The light they create is a very efficient light, or "cold

Comb jellies, which are actually a type of plankton, make bright pulses of light when they are disturbed.

4

light." This means that bioluminescent organisms produce mostly light and almost no heat. A regular incandescent light bulb makes more heat than light.

Some organisms that glow use biofluorescence (pronounced bye-oh-floo-res-uhns). These organisms absorb light from another source, such as the Sun, and then reemit that light as a different color. Usually, these creatures glow green or red. Scientists are studying ways to use fluorescence in science and medicine. Whether they are bioluminescent or use biofluorescence, organisms that glow in the dark are fascinating to see!

In normal light, this deep-sea coral doesn't look unusual. But, under a special light filter, it fluoresces green.

HOW DOES BIOLUMINESCENCE WORK?

Bioluminescent organisms make their own light through a chemical reaction in their bodies. A chemical reaction is a process in which one or more substances are changed to one or more different substances. The reactions that allow organisms to create light require the element oxygen and two special chemicals. One is a substance called luciferin. The other is an enzyme called luciferase. Luciferin reacts with oxygen to create energy in

Up close, this is what the luciferase enzyme of a type of marine bacteria would look like.

THINK ABOUT IT

Fireflies can control how long and how often they flash their light. Why is this important?

the form of light. Luciferase triggers the reaction between the oxygen and luciferin.

Some organisms, including fireflies, also use energy from a substance called adenosine triphosphate, or ATP, to make light. All living things, including people, get energy from the ATP in their cells. Fireflies and many other organisms can regulate their chemistry. This lets them control when they light up and how long their light lasts.

Each type of firefly has its own pattern of flashes. Fireflies use the flashes to attract a mate.

FLYING NIGHT LIGHTS

In many places, fireflies are a familiar sight on summer nights. Sometimes called lightning bugs, fireflies are an insect belonging to the beetle family. There are about 2,000 species, or kinds, of fireflies in the world. Because some adult females and all young fireflies lack wings, they are sometimes called glowworms. Fireflies generally like warm, humid areas, but some live in dry

In most firefly species, males have a larger light organ than females.

8

places. Most fireflies blink to attract mates. Usually the male flashes and waits for a female to flash back.

Each species has its own special pattern of flashes, like a secret code. Fireflies may flash in yellow, orange, or green, but all members of the same species flash the same color. Some species fly together in large numbers, so the females have a hard time seeing the males' flashes. To help the females see them better, male fireflies flash synchronously. Females flash back on their own.

By flashing at the same time, male fireflies help females spot them. Only a few species flash synchronously.

GLOWWORMS AREN'T REALLY WORMS!

Bioluminescent larvae of beetles can't fly. People used to mistake them for worms, so they were called glowworms.

Many types of glowworms live around the world. They may look like small worms but don't be fooled! Most glowworms are larvae of beetles or wingless adult females. In 2014 glowworms of an unknown type of click beetle were found in a Peruvian rainforest. These larvae hide just underground, using their bioluminescent light to lure termites, ants, and other insects. Then they

COMPARE AND CONTRAST

In what ways are these two types of glowworms different? How are they the same?

burst from the ground to snap them up and eat them.

In Australia and New Zealand, some glowworms are the larvae of a tiny fly called a fungus gnat. They light up caves with their bluish glow. But they catch their prey like spiders! The glowworms attach multiple silk threads to the cave roof. Each thread is dotted with beads of sticky mucus. Insects that fly toward the glowworms' lights are trapped in the sticky lines, which are called snares.

Visitors go to the Waitomo Caves in New Zealand to see the dazzling blue glowworms.

CREEPY CRAWLIES THAT GLOW

Some other land creatures that glow include centipedes, millipedes, and earthworms. One type of centipede in tropical Asia glows separately from each of its many segments. At least 10 species of millipedes glow to let predators know they taste bad.

Two known earthworm species ooze a bioluminescent slime. The slime is blue

Bioluminescent millipedes are found in California.

in some species and orange in others. Some scientists think the glowing slime startles predators. This gives the worm time to burrow underground to safety.

The South American railroad worm is unique because its body produces two different colors. On each side of its body, it glows greenish-yellow. The worm also flashes a red light from its head if it feels threatened.

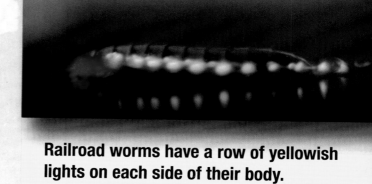

Railroad worms have a row of yellowish lights on each side of their body.

EERIE LIGHTS IN THE WOODS

At night, glowing fungi light up tree trunks in the rainforest at Atherton Tablelands in Queensland, Australia.

Scientists say more than 70 types of fungi are bioluminescent. Although we can only see their light after dark, these fungi glow 24 hours a day. Bioluminescence provides some **antioxidant** protection to fungi. The light also attracts insects that may help spread the spores, so more fungi will grow. Scientists do not know why some fungi glow but others do not.

Aristotle, a Greek scientist and philosopher, wrote about foxfire in the 300s BCE. Foxfire refers to the light from fungi growing on rotting wood. These fungi glow faintly in eerie shades of blue-green, green, or yellow. Two well-known examples are the jack-o'-lantern mushroom and the ghost fungus. Jack-o'-lantern mushrooms are bright yellow-orange— even on the inside. They grow in Europe and North America. Ghost fungus is a white mushroom found in southern Australia. Both are poisonous to people.

Early New England settlers used foxfire to help them find their way through the woods at night.

SWIMMING LIGHTS

Because sunlight only reaches about 656 feet (200 meters) into the ocean, many sea organisms developed the ability to make their own light. Some sea creatures use their light to find prey. One deep-sea octopus emits a bright blue light from some of its suckers. It is thought the octopus uses this light to lure its prey. Firefly

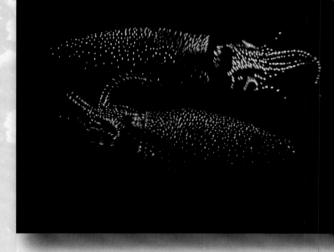

Firefly squid live off the coast of Japa These tiny squid are just 3 inches (7 centimeters) long!

COMPARE AND CONTRAST

Each of these creatures uses light to catch prey. In what ways are they different from each other?

squid flash their lights off and on to attract small fish. Then they grab the fish with their tentacles.

Dragonfish have a light organ called a barbel. It hangs from the chin like a whisker. The dragonfish flashes its light off and on and wiggles its barbel. When small crustaceans and fish come close, the dragonfish snaps them up with its sharp, pointy teeth. Dwarf lantern sharks are only about 7 inches (17.8 centimeters) long. The light on their bellies works like a lantern to attract krill, shrimp, and small fish.

Dragonfish are hard to see underwater. They attract prey by waving their barbel.

DISTRACTED BY THE LIGHT

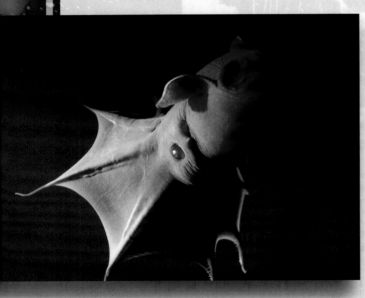

The arms of vampire squid are connected with a web of skin that looks like a cape.

Many organisms use bioluminescence to distract their enemies. Several types of sea worms drop small "bombs" that burst into glowing green light. These "bombs" are actually parts of their bodies that are bioluminescent. Some deep-sea shrimp distract predators by spitting bioluminescent slime at them. Vampire squid squirt mucus from the tips of their tentacles.

THINK ABOUT IT

Some organisms use light to distract their predators. Others use light to get attention. How does each way help protect them?

In each case, the glow lasts long enough for the creature's escape.

Dinoflagellates are tiny one-celled organisms. When bothered, they light up. Their flash of light startles most predators. It also acts like a warning alarm. Predators of the dinoflagellates seem to know that the bright light attracts *their* predators. So they leave before they get caught. The Atolla jellyfish is usually red, a color most sea animals cannot see. But when predators come near, it flashes a bright blue warning alarm.

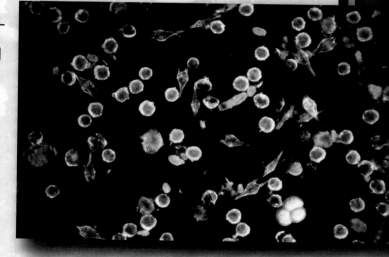

Dinoflagellates are a type of plankton that float on the ocean. They use their bioluminescent light to defend themselves.

AN INVISIBILITY CLOAK

F irefly squid not only use their light to attract prey, they also use light to disappear! By flashing their light in different patterns, firefly squid can disguise their shape. This makes them hard to see. Hatchet fish have thin silver bodies shaped like a hatchet blade. They can make the lights on their bellies brighter or softer.

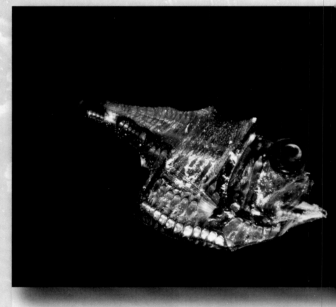

When enemies swimming below hatchet fish look up, all the predator sees is pattern of light because of counter-illumination.

COMPARE AND CONTRAST

Compare how these organisms use bioluminescence to hide. In what ways do they use light differently?

By adjusting their glow to match light coming from above them, they fade from sight. This is called counter-illumination.

Dragonfish often eat other bioluminescent fish. To hide that glow from their predators while they are digesting their food, dragonfish have a black stomach. Loosejaw fish make red light, which most deep-sea organisms cannot see. This lets the loosejaw stay hidden while it hunts.

Loosejaws live in deep, dark water. Their red light helps them hunt for prey without being seen.

TEAM WORK

Hawaiian Bobtail squid live in **symbiosis** with bioluminescent bacteria. The squid feeds the bacteria. In return, the bacteria light up the squid's body. This provides counter-illumination that keeps the squid safe. Flashlight fish also host glowing bacteria. The bacteria live in light organs just under the eyes of the fish. This helps the fish find prey and confuse its predators.

Anglerfish have two kinds of symbiotic relationships. Bioluminescent bacteria in their lure

Bioluminescent bacteria help Hawaiian Bobtail squid blend in with the light above them.

Symbiosis **is a close living arrangement between two different species. Often—but not always—this is helpful to both organisms.**

helps the anglerfish attract prey, and the fish gives the bacteria a place to live. There is also a symbiotic relationship among the males and females of certain types of anglerfish. These male anglerfish are much smaller than the females. Once it matures, the male anglerfish must attach itself to the side of a female or else it dies. The male then depends on the female for survival.

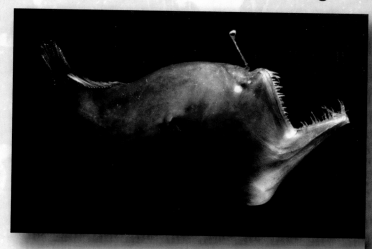

The light in an anglerfish's lure comes from bioluminescent bacteria. Scientists don't know how the bacteria enter the lure.

BIOFLUORESCENCE

Organisms that fluoresce do not make their light. Instead, they take in light of one color from around them and use it to emit, or give off, another color. Usually, high-energy blue light is reemitted as lower-energy green, red, or orange light. On land, fluorescence has been seen in parrots, butterflies, and spiders.

Scorpionfish use fluorescence to blend in with coral. This helps them hide from predators.

THINK ABOUT IT

Bigger, stronger male mantis shrimp have larger patches than smaller males. How does the size of their fluorescent patch help the shrimp?

In the ocean, corals, jellyfish, and more than 180 species of fish use biofluorescence. Scientists think fish use fluorescence to help find mates while staying hidden from predators. Some types of mantis shrimp use biofluorescence to communicate. These mantis shrimp have bright yellow patches on their shell. They use these fluorescent patches to attract mates and to threaten rivals.

Most mantis shrimp are biofluorescent on some parts of their body, but not all mantis shrimp have patches on their shells.

USING BIO-LIGHTS IN MEDICINE AND SCIENCE

Green fluorescent protein can be copied and inserted into other organisms to make them glow.

Organisms that fluoresce have a special protein. Proteins are substances found in many foods and in all living things. They are essential to life. Scientists first found a green fluorescent protein, called GFP, in crystal jellyfish. Later, green, red, and blue fluorescent proteins were found in coral. Scientists can make copies of fluorescent proteins and put them into organisms that do not usually glow. Then, under special light,

COMPARE AND CONTRAST

Fluorescent proteins can be inserted into organisms to make them glow. Compare the ways these proteins are used in medical research. How are scientists using the proteins differently?

the organisms fluoresce. Experiments using fluorescent proteins are helping researchers find new ways to treat diabetes, cancer, and many other diseases!

Some scientists are experimenting to see if they can also make plants and trees glow. Scientists in California plan to insert bioluminescent genes into plants, which would allow the plants to continue glowing as they grew. If scientists can create glowing trees, cities could use them in place of streetlights. That would save energy and look better, too!

GFP found in crystal jellyfish is helping researchers treat certain kinds of disease.

SOMETHING TO GLOW ABOUT

Glowing organisms have fascinated people for thousands of years. Now, studies using fluorescent proteins are helping doctors learn how many diseases work. Scientists hope this will help them develop vaccines to prevent some diseases and find cures for other diseases. Other scientists are looking for ways to use living lights to save energy or to help the environment.

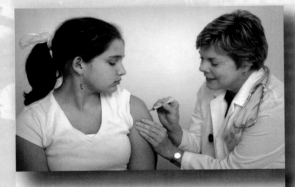

Fluorescent proteins have helped scientists create new vaccines to keep people healthy.

THINK ABOUT IT

Scientists are still learning many things about organisms that glow. Can you think of some other ways in which bioluminescence might be useful?

There is still a lot to learn. For example, scientists don't know why some mushrooms and jellyfish glow while others do not. Scientists are still discovering new species of organisms that glow. In 2015, researchers announced the discovery of a new species of anglerfish in the Gulf of Mexico. All three female fish were less than 4 inches (10 cm) long—much smaller than most species of anglerfish. Scientists believe there are still many glowing organisms waiting to be found. Who knows what they will find next?

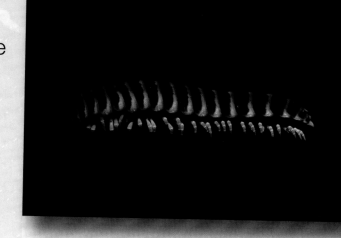

Scientists keep discovering organisms that glow. There is still much to learn about these amazing creatures!

GLOSSARY

ATP A chemical substance in all living things that releases energy.

BACTERIA Tiny, one-celled organisms that are found nearly everywhere.

BARBEL A thin sensory organ on the mouth or chin area of a fish.

CELLS Tiny units that are the basic building blocks of living things. They carry out the basic functions of life either alone or in groups.

COUNTER-ILLUMINATION A method of camouflage in which an organism uses light to blend in with a lighted background.

CRUSTACEANS Animals, such as shrimp, crabs, and lobsters, with a hard outer shell and two pairs of antennas.

ENERGY A source of power that makes something work.

ENZYME A substance that triggers or speeds up a chemical reaction.

FUNGUS A type of living thing, such as yeast, mold, mildew, and mushrooms, that is neither a plant nor an animal.

INCANDESCENT Glowing with intense heat.

LARVAE Wingless young insects that have a wormlike appearance.

LUCIFERASE An enzyme that causes luciferin to combine with oxygen to make light in an organism.

LUCIFERIN A substance that combines with oxygen to make light in an organism.

MUCUS A slimy or gooey substance produced by the body that is usually sticky.

SNARES Traps used to catch prey.

FOR MORE INFORMATION

Books

Bang, Molly, and Penny Chisholm. *Ocean Sunlight: How Tiny Plants Feed the Seas*. New York, NY: Blue Sky Press, 2012.

Beck, W. H. *Glow: Animals with Their Own Night-Lights*. Boston MA: HMH Books for Young Readers, 2015.

De Bedoyere, Camilla, and Steve Parker. *300 Fantastic Facts: Oceans: Your Guide to the Marine World*. Thaxted, England: Miles Kelly, 2014.

Howell, Sara. *Fireflies*. New York, NY: PowerKids Press, 2015.

Jenkins, Steve. *The Beetle Book*. Boston, MA: HMH Books for Young Readers, 2012.

Leaf, Christina. *Anglerfish*. Minneapolis, MN: Bellwether Media, 2014.

Rajczak, Kristen. *Glowworms*. New York, NY: PowerKids Press, 2015

Websites

Because of the changing nature of Internet links, Rosen Publishing has developed an online list of websites related to the subject of this book. This site is updated regularly. Please use this link to access this list:

http://www.rosenlinks.com/NMY/glow

INDEX